PUPPYDOG BLUES

By Marshall Silverman

Illustrated by Andres Mignucci
Graphic Layout by Laura Jaramillo

TO SUZANNE:

YOU INVARIABLY HELP ME SEE THE
NRECOGNIZED PATTERN IN EACH NEW
HAPTER WE SCRIPT. AND TO OBSERVE
ACH DETAIL INLAID WITHIN THE TEXT.
VEN TYPICAL DEDICATIONS STRANGLEY
IMILAR TO PLAYFUL ONES LIKE THIS
AN HAVE SPECIAL MEANING. THANK YOU
UZANNE FOR GIVING ME MY INSPIRATION.

TABLE OF CONTENTS

MY LIZARD

My lizard passed away today.
I think. It's hard to tell.
Lizards often rarely move
For quite a lengthy spell.

The crickets we've been feeding him
Are hopping on his head.
Mom says, "He's not hungry."
Dad says, " 'Cause he's dead."

His body's cold. He doesn't blink.
His skin is rough and cracked.
In every way he's acting like
A lizard ought to act.

And yet I have this feeling that
He's perfectly unwell.
My lizard passed away today.
I think. It's hard to tell.

PADDLING

A family of four tried to paddle to shore.
They paddled with skill and with heart.
Each stroke was rehearsed, from the last to the first:
A choreographed work of art.

Despite their display as they paddled that day
There was never a hope for the crew.
This family of four had each brought an oar,
But none of them brought the canoe.

ON HEARING MY YOUNGER BROTHER
IS MOVING INTO MY ROOM

Never mind the Mummies
That sleep beneath my floor.
Never mind the Monsters
I find behind my door.

Never mind the Goblins
That hide inside my light.
And never mind the Frankenstein
That visits every night.

Never mind the Specter
Within my window pane.
Never mind the Zombie.
It's clear he's near-insane.

My room is getting crowded.
Whatever. Never mind.
But letting *him* move in with me?
That's where I draw the line!

WEEKLY
CHORES

Feed the porch
And sweep my fishes.
Wash the lawn
And mow the dishes.

Paint the dog
And walk the shed.
Make-up the trash
Then take out my bed.

Obey my toys.
Pick up my mother.
Be nice to the garden
And weed my brother.

I do my chores.
I don't resist.
Dad says next week
Make a LIST!

DIAMONDS IN THE ROUGHAGE

I found an emerald in my peas -
A ruby in my beets.
A pearl appeared inside my cheese;
        Such unexpected treats!

This bowl of corn has chunks of gold
-A diamond's in my ice.
I don't like karats, hot or cold;
        But these are rather nice!

I'd like to compliment the cook –
This food's beyond belief.
It's easy on my pocket book;
        But murder on my teeth!

BIRTHDAY PRESENTS

Today has been a birthday
Unlike my birthdays past,
Each present that I opened
Was stranger than the last.

My mom made me a cheesecake
Entirely of stone.
My dad went out and bought me
A velvet saxophone.

My uncle gave me acorns.
My aunt sent me a pack
Of solar-powered boomerangs.
(I had to send them back.)

My younger sister gift-wrapped
Some water in a box.
The twins agreed to give me
A pair of chocolate socks.

My friends all pulled together
And bought me half a yacht.
I tell you, I'm astounded
By all the gifts I got.

I don't know where they rummaged
Or where they bargain-hunted,
But this year I got everything
I'd ever said I wanted.

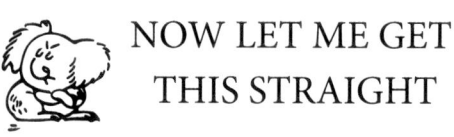

NOW LET ME GET
THIS STRAIGHT

Koala Bears aren't really bears.
The Pole Cat's not a cat.
The famous furry Flying Fox
Is actually a bat.

The Groundhog and the Guinea Pig
Are neither pigs nor hogs.
The Wombat's not a bat at all,
And Prairie Dogs aren't dogs.

The Glow Worm is a firefly.
The Ring Worm is a yeast.
The Horny Toad's a lizard
And not toadlike in the least.

The Silkworm and the Silver Fish
Are insects through and through.
The Seahorse is no horse, I'm told –
And Sea Cows never moo.

I don't know who's responsible
For picking out these names,
But certainly this Brainiac
Did not have any brains.

EXCAVATOR

I hear there's a Beast on the lot down the street.
He's gobbling greedily all he can eat.

His jaws are relentless; his breath is black smoke.
His diet is mainly red maple and oak.

He grazes on gravel – and once, for dessert,
I heard he devoured an acre of dirt.

I don't know what keeps him from leaving that lot.
Perhaps that's his home or perhaps – it is not.

They say, on that lot, they'll build houses – but please,
That Thing is still roving and ripping up trees.

Before they start building I think that, at least,
They need to decide how to deal with that Beast!

BELLY FLOP

My pond is dry
As desert sand.
No H-2-Oh,
Just dry dry land.

The fish that swam
(As fishies must)
Are sadly flapping
In the dust.

There's nothing wet
For man or horse.
The frogs are hopping
Mad, of course.

I watched my pond
Lose every drop
The day Granddaddy
Belly Flopped.

EYEBROWS

Don't ask me how it happened.
I swear I barely blinked.
My eyebrows now are missing.
They're gone. Kaput. Extinct.

I saw them just this morning
Appearing quite content.
They showed no sign of leaving
I don't know where they went.

They did not ask permission.
There was no ransom note,
And no negotiation.
I did not get a vote.

I'm coping with their absence.
My newest exercise
Is training caterpillars
To STAY above my eyes.

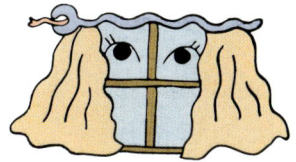

LIVING ROOM

The sofa's snoring soundly.
The armchair's laying eggs.
The coffee table's creeping off
    On animated legs.

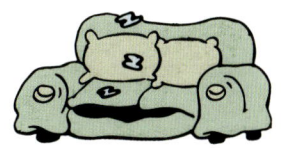

All the walls are breathing.
The windows are awake.
The curtain rods are writhing like
    An anaconda snake.

The carpet is cavorting.
The piano's playing chase.
The mantle is meandering
    Beneath the fireplace.

All my friends have houses
    As quiet as a tomb.
I'm sure that mine's the only home
    That has a Living Room.

And if that were not strange enough
    To drive a boy to tears –
I've not gone in the *Dining* Room
    For twelve or thirteen years.

THE BUTTON

In my basement
On a chair
Under dust
Over there,

In a safebox
Locked up tight
There's a Button
Plain and white.

Round and heavy,
Warm to hold
Labeled clearly
Black and bold,

Saying simply,
"Listen kid,
Under no circumstances should you push this button
or your bossy big sister will disappear."

And she did.

A THUNDERSTORM

A thunderstorm is in my mouth.
It's rained in there for weeks.
The wind is whistling through my teeth
And puffing out my cheeks.

Each jagged bolt of lightning leaves
My lips as chapped as chalk.
I've swallowed so much water that
I'm sloshing when I walk.

It's not what I expected and
I think I ought to know.
Especially since the weatherman
Had promised it would snow.

BULLFROG

What do you do when your Bullfrog's perplexed?
Befuddled, befroggled, and otherwise vexed?

Dreaming odd dreams of Mexican shores.
Of cows and of crowds and of mad matadors?

What do you do when you cannot wear red,
For fear you'll provoke him to lower his head?

He'll snort and he'll stamp and he'll stomp quite a lot,
Preparing to gore you with horns he has not.

We've tried talking sense to his bullheaded brain.
We're not so convinced he's entirely sane.

The odds he'll recover are slimmer than slim.
It's heartache for us and a headache for him.

A HEAD WILL NOT FIT

A head will not fit in the mailbox.
Amazing but true, nonetheless.
The head, it appears,
Is too big at the ears.
A flaw in design, I confess.

Nor will it fit in the fishtank.
This I've attempted discretely.
The snag, I suppose,
Is the bridge of the nose,
Which keeps it from sliding in neatly.

The washing machine and the hamper,
The mouth of a frog opened wide -
Are all the wrong fit
I'm forced to admit
For the head of a person inside.

But a two-gallon pail on the noggin
Will faithfully fit where you've stuck it.
The problem, in fact,
Is how to extract
Your kid brother's head from a bucket.

MY HOUSE

My house is your typical house I suppose
With counters for cooking and closets for clothes.

The seventeen attics are standard I think,
Along with your average ice skating rink.

The archery range is of basic design.
You'll find it beneath the uranium mine.

The egg-dipping spa is like yours, I assume.
It's just down the hall from the hang-gliding room.

The barbeque pit (with retractable dome)
Of course is a feature that came with the home.

The train ticket office and snowboarding lodge
Are where you'd expect them, behind the garage.

It's not that my house is abnormal or queer,
It's just that there's nothing to do around here.

CROCODILE IN MY DRAWER

A crocodile's in my drawer.
I'm shocked - I'm overcome.
I cannot find my undershirts.
I almost lost my thumb.

She's hoarding all my bathing suits.
I think she's built a nest.
It's getting downright dangerous
Attempting to get dressed.

I've never bothered much to care
How crocodiles felt,
But still, I hope she doesn't find
  That alligator belt.

Each day it's getting harder to
Insure my socks are matching –
I'd better sort out something soon,
I think her eggs are hatching.

BAGGY SOCKS

My socks are loose and baggy.
They refuse to hold their shape.
Despite my use of rubberbands
And double-sided tape.

Every method I've employed
To minimize the slippage
Has met with limited success
From insufficient grippage.

I've tried and tied each boyscout knot
With little bits of twine.
I've integrated Velcro
In a patented design.

Airplane glue and pine tar
Aren't as sticky as they seem.
The staples and the thumbtacks
Were a bloody stupid scheme.

The bubble gum and Band Aids
Were a fashion near-disaster.
No longer can I recommend
Concrete, cement, or plaster.

Though more important issues
Surely plague humanity.
The problem is more serious
For centipedes like me.

BROKEN

My brother broke his pinky toe.
He made an awful fuss.
They wouldn't send an ambulance,
We couldn't find a bus.

Our car was sadly in the shop.
No cab would come our way.
But when my brother broke his toe,
A toe-truck saved the day!

ANTLINE

Marching crunching

        stamping   stomping

            chomping munching Wait!

                  Stop bunching.

            Zipping   zopping

      flipping   flopping

   rolln-rocking.   You!

No stopping!

    Bumping whirling

  twirling thumping

    weaving

      swerving

           -up (boy that's unnerving).

      downside-

              Clicking clacking

        now backtracking

  hustling bustling   in a tizzy

turning curving

      Whew! I'm d^{i}z

LITTLE MONSTER

First he ripped off both the arms
And ate them with a snort.
Next he gobbled up the ears
Apparently for sport.

With undiminished appetite
He slurped up both the eyes.
And when he nibbled off the nose
It came as no surprise.

He gently prodded at the legs
Before he gnawed them off.
The lips were last to find their way
Into his feeding trough.

The sad remains were batted 'round
Then wedged beneath his bed.
And that is what our poodle did
To Mr. Potato Head.

PUPPYDOG BLUES

I found my goldfish downside-uppie.
Mom said, "Shoulda gotta guppy."
All I wanted was a puppy.
I got them dead-fish blues.

Has anybody seen my froggy?
The toilet musta made him groggy.
This wouldn't happen to a doggy.
I got them flush-frog blues.

This gerbil is so squeaky-squeally.
Spends all day inside his wheelly
But even he can't outrun, really,
Them whirling-gerbil blues.

Look, it's no perplexing puzzle.
One end's Wag the other's Muzzle.
All this heartache just becuzzle
I got them puppydog blues.

THADDEUS
THOUGHTFULLY

Thaddeus thoughtfully thought for a spell.
He pondered and wondered and reckoned as well.

He stopped to consider, imagine and mull,
And judge every option that entered his skull.

He mused and conceived; and he'd think long and hard –
And then ruminate and reflect and regard.

He'd cogitate, contemplate, speculate too,
Meditate, study and weigh points of view.

His thoughts were as thick as the trees in a forest,
Since Thaddeus thoughtfully ate that thesaurus.

I've looked in the closet and hamper.
I've checked in the bathtub and sink.
And here's what I know:
He's nowhere I go,
And nowhere I know where to think.

He's not underneath the credenza.
And the curtains, I'm certain I've checked.
It's eerie to me
How he's able to be
Everywhere I don't see or suspect.

I'm sure he is not in the cushions.
I've inspected each cranny and nook.
It's always the way
In this game that we play
That he'll be in the last place I look.

One thing I have learned from my trials:
Success in this game all depends
On flawless technique
If you play Hide and Seek
With invented, invisible friends.

CAT EGGS

My kitty laid a dozen eggs
Right on the kitchen floor.
It shocked us all for certain, but
It shocked my kitty more.

We called the local paper, and
We called the Guiness Book.
We asked the felinologist
To come and have a look.

The experts cried, "Impossible!"
"This has to be a ploy."
"Of course your cat cannot lay eggs,
This kitty-cat's a boy."

STATUE

I'm a statue.
I'm a fixture.
I'm a monolithic stone.
I do not move a muscle as
I stand here all alone.

Tides may ebb
And tides may flow,
And kingdoms rise and fall -
While I remain immobile
At the center of it all.

Set my hair on fire and
    I will not even flinch.
Tickle, tease, or torture me
And I'll not budge an inch.

They'll put me in the record book
For standing still and straight.
Already I've stood motionless
A minute-forty-eight.

YELLING BEE

Barbara barked barbarian
As loud as she could blare.
Aardvark answered Anthony
With decibels to spare.

Harold hollered *horticulture.*
Hugh howled *homicide.*
Waldo whispered *wombat* and
He was disqualified.

Cory roared out *corrugated.*
Susan screamed *surcease.*
The cops gave both a ticket
For disturbance of the peace.

As Barbara's turn came 'round again
A voice from upstairs said,
"I'll superglue your tonsils if
You kids don't go to bed."

I guess a slumber party
At a quarter after three
Is not the time nor place to stage
The County Yelling Bee.

OVERALL OTIS

No matter how madly he hunted and chased,
Overall Otis could not find his waist.

Overall, life was easy or so Otis felt.
Unless he attempted to buckle his belt.

Then it was hard, overall, not to notice
The crumpled up pants at the ankles of Otis.

Regardless of what, overall, was to blame,
The answer was basically plain as his name.

SOFA BED

I had a very peaceful night
Upon your sofa bed.
I snoozed and snored all snug and tight
While dreams danced through my head.

This morning I awoke to find I
couldn't breathe the air.
My arms and legs were in a bind
And Dark was everywhere.

I lay, unmoving, for a time.
'Til hunger hit my lips.
Then luckily I found a dime
And three potato chips.

I'm not some grim, ungrateful grouch.
My days *have* started worse.
But next time you fold up your couch
Perhaps you'll wake me first?

KUDZU

We grow green and swing on vine.
We climb pole and power line.
We're tight.
We're true.
Kudzu.

We tumble green down mountainside.
We cover signs that seek to hide.
We can.
We do.
Kudzu.

We slither green. We crawl and creep,
Then pounce on fence and rusted jeep
We know
Kung-fu.
Kudzu.

We cling green like slimy sneeze.
We fling ourself on helpless trees.
We stick
Like glue
Kudzu!

GAS-STATION GUS

Gas-station Gussie lived up to his name:
The best car mechanic in all of the game.

With naught but a wrench and a small tuning fork,
He'd boost your ignition and beef up your torque.

There wasn't an engine he couldn't adjust.
Such were the talents of Gas-station Gus.

He'd work night and day 'til each job was complete,
Pausing but briefly to wash up and eat.

Each meal he'd have beans and drink Coke by the glass,
    - Explaining how Gas-station Gus got his gas.

PENNY LOAFERS

I put a penny in my shoe,
And in my shoe it went.
I found it in my time of need:
I called it heaven-cent.

I put a penny in my shoe,
With practical intents.
The shoes were penny loafers so
It seemed like common cents.

I put a penny in my shoe.
The money was well spent.
My shoes were sadly stinky and
Deserved a pleasant cent.

I paid a penny for my thoughts.
I took it from my shoe.
I gave it to a friend in need:
The de-cent thing to do.

WALKING CIRCLES

I'm walking in circles
Around and around.
Retracing and pacing
The same patch of ground.

I'm not deviating
At all from my route.
Not one smidgen inward,
Nor one inchward out.

My method of marching,
I simply will state,
Is mostly a matter
Of not walking straight.

You too can walk circles
There's nothing to lose.
Just start walking Leftward
Or Right, if you choose.

But please don't distract me,
There's no time to spare.
I've places to get and
I'm just about there.

EAT YOUR VEGGIES

The broccoli
Is stalking me.
It's nothing I can prove.
I'm sure *those*
Aren't "sweet" potatoes
That eye my every move.

That cabbage
Is a savage.
I think it wants my head.
The lettuce
Vowed to get us
When I'm sleeping in my bed.

The corn has ears,
It snoops and hears
It's gone starch-raving mad.
The succotash
Is talking trash -
It's mixed up really bad.

This smorgasbord
Is off its gourd!
So what's a kid to do?
The message here
Is loud and clear
Eat your veggies or, I fear,
They'll end up eating you!

SUPERNOVA

My fish went supernova.
Man did he explode!
Gills and guts went flying
Clear across the road.

He always seemed high-strungish
I know it makes no sense.
At least he is at present
Undoubtedly past tense.

My fish went supernova.
And blasted through the wall.
I guess I'm not surprised – He was
A starfish afterall.

I'M DIGGING

I'm digging a hole in the sand on the beach.
I'm digging whatever my shovel will reach.

I don't have a purpose. I don't have a plan.
I'm flailing and bailing as fast as I can.

There's sand on my hands and there's sand in my suit.
There's sand where I stand in my sandals, to boot.

I figure I'll dig for a good little bit.
I think I'll be finished whenever I quit.

So far what I've flung to the sea from the shore,
Has filled up the ocean. The ocean's no more.

I don't have a motive or message to teach -
Just digging a hole in the sand on the beach.

GRANNY HOLLERS

When Granny hollers like a pig,
Pigs come runnin' hard.
When Granny hollers like a bear,
Bears fill up her yard.

When Granny hollers like a bull,
They charge with steady speed.
When Granny hollers like a moose,
She starts a moose-stampede.

When Granny hollers like a sphinx,
A yeti or a gnome,
They all wink into being
And follow Granny home.

When Granny gets to hollerin'
The critters can't say No.
We're hoping one day Granny learns
The trick to make them Go.

46

MY STUPID DOG

My stupid dog was doggedly
In circular pursuit.
His prey was tantalizingly
Mere inches from his snoot.

With sheer determination he
Eventually prevailed
In chasing down and catching his
Poor unsuspecting tail.

He swallowed nearly half of it
Before it crossed his mind
The thing that wagged in front of him
Was really his behind.

IN THE FRIDGE

My legs have lost all feeling.
My joints have stiffened too.
There's goosebumps on my goosebumps
And my lips are turning blue.

The smell of mozzarella
Is grating on my nerves.
That pain in my left kidney
Is a jar of peach preserves.

I've been here for an hour -
Could be another four.
Who knew there was no handle
On the inside of the door?

At least I've got the evidence
Which proves beyond a doubt
That when the fridge's door is shut
The little light goes out.

MIXED GREENS

This garden I'm growing is growing just fine.
With ripe cantemelon and spuds on the vine.

My prize cucaloupes are the largest I've seen.
I'm awfully proud of my fresh boysenbeans.

I've stringbeets and pumpkorn and waterdew too.
(My crop of okrumber is sadly quite few).

There's cabbuce and lettage and even tomaddish.
My squashberries make me especially gladdish.

But next time I'm planting what my garden needs
I must take more care not to mix up my seeds!

SHUTTING UP

"I've nothing left to say
And that's a cold and honest fact.
I might as well reveal
The conversation that I lack.

I've said what's on my mind:
You'll kindly mind what I have said.
There's no more useful verbage
Apt to issue from my head.

I guess that I'll be quiet,
Since no words are left to speak.
It's certain you won't hear me
Talking on and on all week.

There's people who don't know
When it is time to shut their yap.
I know you know I know
To never fall into that trap.

My lips are locked and zippered,
And I've thrown the key away.
I tell you I'm not talking.
I have nothing left to say . . ."

PROPER ATTIRE

Victoria Carly
Would dress for the day
In Proper Attire
For work or for play.

A jumper for jumping,
Pajamas for naps,
Some sneakers for sneaking,
And always – Three caps.

A sweater for sweating,
One scarf too, perhaps,
One tu-tu for dancing,
And always – Three caps.

Some days called for zippers,
And others for snaps,
Or buckles or buttons,
But always – Three caps.

It's simply a matter,
Victoria said,
Of Proper Attire:
One cap for each head.

DAD'S TRUCK

Wrinkled, wrecked and rusted,
Its wheels are bald as brass.
The radiator's busted.
We think it's leaking gas.

    It belches smoke and thunder.
    The parking brake is gone.
    The bumper's bending under.
    The blinker's always on.

The seats are torn and tattered.
The heater doesn't blow.
And any knob that mattered
Fell off a while ago.

    We haven't changed the anti-freeeze
    Since 1955.
    And dad says I can have the keys
    As soon as I can drive!

CAMEL

My dromedary disappeared,
Deserting me as darkness neared.

Evading me, he ducked and dodged,
Alas, he was well-camelflaged.

CRYING KNIGHT

I am the armored Crying Knight.
I'm sensitive and smart.
If you have damsels in distress
It breaks my weeping heart.

I tend to cry a river when
Confronted with my fears.
No fire-breathing dragon can
Withstand my tide of tears.

Magicians of the blackest art
Surrender if they're wise.
Rather than be swept away
Before my streaming eyes.

My deeds are damp and dangerous.
My valor I would prove;
Except my armor's rusted through
And now I cannot move.

WHATEVER

We found the Bridge to Apathy
But please don't ask us where.
We did not bring a map and we
Quite frankly do not care.

BACKWARDING FRIDAY

I just saw the cat chase my doggie away.
The dog then commanded my father to stay.
There's something amiss.
I've heard about this.
It's gotta be Backwarding Friday today.

Homework gets done only after we play.
Dessert precedes dinner – a chocolate souffle'.
From all that I hear
It's stranger each year.
It's gotta be Backwarding Friday today.

Coaches and teachers must fully obey
The slightest suggestion each student might say.
The chaos begins
Right after it ends.
It's gotta be Backwarding Friday today.

Only the Chicken and egg seem okay.
Our cow and her milk are in utter dismay.
It's truly bizzaro.
I'm glad that tommorow
It changes to Upside Down Saturday day.

KIDDIE POOL

Who put that pesky Killer Whale
Inside the kiddie-pool?
It's downright irresponsible,
Unthinkable, and cruel.

A kiddie-pool is not the spot
For Killer Whales to wait.
He might get claustrophobic
And hyperventilate.

This water's way too shallow.
The sun'll burn his back.
    And any food he's apt to find
        Is just a kiddie-snack.

    A kiddie-pool is not some zoo,
        Or fancy water-park
        So please remove that Killer Whale –
          He's bothering the Shark.

FLOPPY JALOPY

The Floppy Jalopy
Impossibly bends.
It sags in the middle
And droops at the ends.

The windows - they wiggle.
The chassis is slack.
And that's a reliable
Pliable fact.

And though you'd be wise
To avoid heavy loads,
It's slinkishly suited
For spiraling roads.

It stretches when starting,
And bobs when it stops.
But mostly the Floppy
Jalopy just . . . flops.

PSEUDO-PLANET

Pluto, pseudo-planet,
You're mostly frozen granite.

Astronomy has voted.
You've sadly been demoted.

Your rank they did abolish
For being over smallish.

PAPA FRITZ

Perplexifying Papa Fritz
Only spoke in opposites.

I'd hear him say that night is day,
That black is white and work is play.

And things he said he liked a lot –
You could be sure he liked them not.

So when he said a big, "Hello"
We knew he meant "It's time to go."

If Papa Fritz declared a drought,
You'd best get your umbrella out.

One day he paused and said to me
"I fail to miss what I don't see."

It's been ten years since that event,
And still I don't know what he meant.

BORROWING BARTLEBY'S

We are the Borrowing Bartleby's
We've nothing of our own.
We borrow all the Luxuries
You're kind enough to loan.

A silken scarf. A matching hat.
We'll borrow, if we may.
A quart of milk to give the cat
We borrowed yesterday.

A magazine. Your favorite books.
We're sorry but we must.
We'll keep them on our shelves for looks,
Collecting borrowed dust.

We are the Borrowing Bartleby's
We show up now and then.
The objects we politely seize
You'll never see again.

A kangaroo. A rubber ball.
A ton of chicken feed.
No item is too large or small
For us to need to need.

And when we need some cash to spend,
Of course, the cash we lack.
We'll gladly borrow what you'll lend
And rarely pay it back.

We are the Borrowing Bartleby's.
The subjects of this rhyme.
And now we'll thank you kindly, please
For lending us your time.

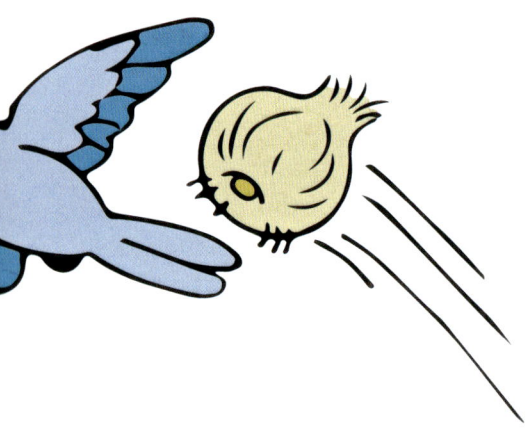

FLINGIN' ONIONS

I'm flingin' onions at the moon.
They say I'm crazy as a loon.
But if I fling my onions right,
We'll have another satellite.

I'm flingin' onions at the moon.
If we should have a June-Monsoon,
It's likely from the pull applied
By my onions on the tide.

I'm flingin' onions at the moon.
I think tomorrow afternoon,
At Saturn I will aim my flings –
'Course I'll be usin' onion rings.

PHANTOM PHILIP PHOTON

I'm Phantom Philip Photon –
Phenomenally phleet.
I move like a Pherrari
On phairly phlying pheet.

I ophten get bephuddled –
Because I am so phast,
I'm phlung into the phuture
Bephore I've lepht the past.

My pholks can never phind me –
I'm too phast to be phound.
Their shouts phall short behind me.
I'm much more phast than sound.

I phinnish all my homework
In halph a nano-sec.
I don't know iph it's accurate –
I phrequently don't check.

My teachers say they'll phail me,
I phake as iph I'm deaph.
They've told me this phorever, and
I've yet to get an "F".

THE END

This is the End of everything.
There's nothing past this place.
There's nothing snappy happening
There simply isn't space.

The total lack of space and time
Is tough to comprehend.
But you can bet your only dime
That Here is where they end.

The stuff that isn't over there
Is really quite a lot.
Nothing there is everywhere,
And Anywhere is not.

So if I move a step or two
And cross this line right here,
Will I slowly fade from view
Or quickly dis . . .

ABOUT THE AUTHOR

Marshall lives in Charlotte, NC, with his beautiful (and tolerant) wife and three teenage kids. His family includes dogs, cats, and fish. They had bunnies and gerbils and lizards for a while. They also had 3 chickens but a weasel ate them.

In addition to writing Children's poetry, Marshall putters at his workbench a lot, plays the violin occasionally, runs marathons sometimes and shaves his head weekly. He has a busy medical practice but he does not give shots to his patients.

He asks his nurse to do that.